THIS
IS
NOT
A
SKY

THIS IS NOT A SKY

JESSICA PIAZZA

Black Lawrence Press

Black Lawrence Press

www.blacklawrence.com

Executive Editor: Diane Goettel
Chapbook Editor: Kit Frick
Book and Cover Design: Amy Freels

Copyright © 2014 Jessica Piazza
ISBN: 978-1-62557-917-1

All rights reserved. Except for brief quotations in critical articles or reviews, no part of this book may be reproduced in any manner without prior written permission from the publisher: editors@blacklawrencepress.com

Published 2014 by Black Lawrence Press.
Printed in the United States.

For my sister soldier, Jill Alexander Essbaum, who helps me see what is sky and what isn't . . .

Contents

Café Terrace at Night
    after Van Gogh   1

School of Athens
    after Raphael   3

Gun
    after Warhol   4

The Treachery of Images
    after Magritte   7

Brouillard à l'Hermitage, Pontoise
    after Pissarro   8

Study for a Bullfight
    after Bacon   9

Adam and Eve
    after Chagall   11

Print Gallery
    after Escher   12

The Fight Between Carnival and Lent
    after Bruegel   13

Rain, Steam and Speed—The Great Western Railway
    after Turner   14

The Great Wave off Kanagawa
    after Hokusai   16

New York Movie
    after Hopper   17

The Persistence of Memory
    after Dalí   18

Two Girls in Black
    after Renoir   19

Blue Nude
    after Picasso   21

Roman Notes
    after Twombley   22

Ophelia
    after Millais   23

Erased de Kooning
    after Rauschenberg   24

Acknowledgments & Notes   25

A Note on the Text

Each of these poems is titled after a famous work of art; the original painters are referenced in the subtitles.

There is a barcode included with each poem and scanning this code with a QR reader will bring you to an image of the painting. Whenever possible, the codes lead to the gallery, museum or collection that owns the painting. When that was not possible, we tried to find the most stable and accessible source available.

Café Terrace at Night
after Van Gogh

The ladies and gentleman, dapper. Astral lanterns glare gaily: the formerly ominous sky, candelabra'd and gilded and precious.

(It's Venice. Or Paris.
                      They're tipsy. They're gorgeous.)

Verandas are paintings for passersby, glaze-eyed, unstumbling, unfazed by the cobblestoned goings. The patrons, bedazzled on red woven rugs, drink café au lait, limoncello, and wine.

(And her? No really . . . she's fine.)

Though the awning's aslant, and the golden patina makes faceless and foregone, a shape of a shadow. A man in a doorway. A man she might know.

(Please go. Please go.)

And the curve of his coat summons thoughts of a lamp glinting harshly off mirrors she'd dampened with gauze. That lowing, that losing. That lowering light.

(One terrible night gives all other nights pause.)

But the stars. The stars. The promenade hours. The weather and color. The memories severed by laughter, its washing, its waves. No one gone, no one grave.

No graves.

School of Athens
after Raphael

The gods and the beasts,
              (twins)—   are the better and the bad
      I searched out.   The massed wheeling circles of the stars
            gain their reputation   from storms and tempest.
And love, composed of   a single soul inhabiting two   bodies,
              (the mathematical thoughts of god)
      is an unfoldment
              I have often regretted.   My speech *(never my silence)*
                       is possible. Nothingness is not:
see: one promontory one mountain   one sea   one river   and see all.
     The moon not a god,   but a great rock   and the sun a hot rock.
               (It is not the same river. He is not the same man.)
Every heart sings a song, incomplete, until another heart whispers back
geometry in the humming of the strings; music in the spacing of the spheres.
               Fire burns only when we are near it.
           Stand a little less between me and the sun.

Gun
after Warhol

When I shot you
        with the black gun
I smugly hummed; I strolled away. How easy it is when you're clean. The gun was the color of every mean deed that I've never done, deep dark of each hate I never plumbed. *(I gathered my honey by watching instead.)* When you slipped into bed, when you tripped on the rug. When you won *(and you always, always won.)* And I shot, but my eyes were closed. And I heard, but I didn't see. And it happened, to a degree. And if it's the truth that you never got dead, it was pleasant to see that I could have succeeded. And pleasant to know how you might have pleaded. And pleasant, your almost screaming. *(The only unpleasant thing? Leaving.)*

When I shot you
>	with the red gun

I did not run, stranded in widening tides of blood, muddled colors flooding the scene *(just so much red on so much red)*, the dread of the object mislaid and unfound. Rising steam occluded the room, and you lied, unmoved, as I shouted and shouted. (*My story, my reasons, my bright quarter hour.*) They hounded me: flashbulbs and friends, assholes, the past *(the told-you-so always a trigger away)* but I stayed, and I stayed, and you never got dead. And inside my highly imaginative head, the crowd's mea culpas deleted my moment of sun. *(And it was no fair. And it was no fun.)*

When I shot you
>with the white gun

I knew you'd come. I fired, you swooned; it shone opal and diamond, a second moon. It was noon, and still glitter and powder and hair. *(I won, but I didn't care.)* The ladies wore boas and nothing else; the beautiful men repeated themselves. And they always will. *(And I'd always hear.)* I did it because you were here. I did it because you cared. I did it because I could. The whizzes and bangs, the voices I measured in inches all called from the one place I couldn't record. But you never got bored. But you never got dead. *(But I did.)*

The Treachery of Images
after Magritte

Neither pipe nor a pipe dream, your shadow's revenge is its ending. No blue revolution and no starry nightmare loosen their hold on the setting. A plain brown board upon which the unnamed object lies. *(This is not a sky.)* Your silence resides between rise of breath and whispers of brush and of stroke. Brooms swish, but no room and the moon is still full of itself, alone. You're home, but the fire's unstoked. *(This is not a joke.)* Air enters your ears; two tails, an impaling. Don't bother. You can't paint your father, can't picture the gore nor gather the smoke. Draw swords or draw blanks or whatever you want, but not falling disaster. *(There isn't an after.)* No nothing that happens, no truth, no act. No apples. *(That's later.)* You've waited. You're nowhere. You've been here? You're only impossibly gone. Not flesh, not eyes. And the wood is dark. And the band is gold. And brown, after all, may be sky. *(This is not a lie.)*

Brouillard à l'Hermitage, Pontoise
after Pissarro

These are the winter
              wanderer's   fetters.

Sopping
            stocking
                      snowbound
                                    march.

The sky's arch
                —menacing
        gunmetal—   threatens;

nemesis and staunch.

It keeps you miles away,
this weather.

                                    (Like you never loved me much.)

Study for a Bullfight
after Bacon

The bull's revenge still ends in running. Goring done,
its triumph dulled by endless going toward enraging red.
                        (God is the bull. God is red. God is the dead
             torero, ended, sweating skin skill steaming.)
Even so, the bull is
gleaming black. Stark pool—panacea,
problem—underneath a faceless matador.
The only red seen: heat-bright highlight captured
in his half-drawn form.
            (No bloody hands, no bloody horns.
                      God is the gore, but God is it gone.)
Are they alone? The sea of eyes that witness
carnage multiplies, enlarges. Unless
each eye is His and no one else is there.
              (No bloodshot stares, no teeming stands.
                  God wants
    what God demands.)
The canvas trusses up the corridor,
arena and its orange walls. The fighter,
fallen, cannot fall. Outside, the painter's
hand is shaking.
          (God is the paint. God is the panting.)
Tainted, all we are is dirt.
            (God is the street

> *and the dawn*

and the hurt.)

Undrawn, the downed man's pain won't even
stain the cobblestones. Gored man, gone bull: both
deaths, a too-small coat.

> *(In screaming, God is the throat.)*

Adam and Eve
after Chagall

Some say the world will end in fire, a pyre the best
      of us watch while the worst are purged, already ashen.

The man I loved loves endings of this sort. (*No ellipses. Small*
      apocalypses limping one after the other

into the light-washed after-morning healing.)
      Imagine us standing silently at the barren

spring lip of a vineyard. The vines are twisted,
      mist over them, like charred hands scratching

the background hills. He is giddy. *(All this*
      illness—thrilling.) Branches black, all of it aching.

Overtaken by this goneness (*his fingers*
      in mine soft and white, malicious), everything feels

finished. Fires untying the knot of us. The burn
      of our own promise. This torture by interminable

smolder, slow inferno. My only wish: that it would end
      for us by ice instead. *(But we're already dead.)*

Print Gallery
after Escher

And the world endlessly curved. And the stairs never went anywhere.
And always, I stayed right here. And always, you stayed very still.

I lived in this gallery. I saw you once, across.
But you seemed endlessly cross, so I only watched you for days.

You leaned toward me, elbows on sill. The boat in the water
tipped. The gondola wasn't ashore. And I wasn't sure anymore.

I never could fill in your face. It might have been me, across.
You were always a cross away, behind each windowpane's wooden T.

And the paintings were mounted on air. I watched you, across, and here.
You were just at the end of the hall. I watched you, impossibly near.

And it's been a hundred years
of windows and windows and walls.

And every escape I might have endeavored, they limit.
      (If there is an outside,
I'm in it.)

The Fight Between Carnival and Lent
after Bruegel

Holy, holy.
        Robes clothing haunches, prayers
for rare debaucheries. This candlelight.
        This fervent want.
(Delight: the shop girl's skirt, too tight.)

        The balustrades house men
enraged, enflamed
        by steamy streaming women
filled with unfulfilling days.
        No meat, no heat, all only no.
(And still the old crone rows, she rows.)

        The vicar slows none in his oaring.
Fat man shored and floated
        downtown
fighting hunched priests,
        crooning, swimming.

(River of bodies dammed with mouths.)
(River of damned unmoored by more.)

        Crawling for scraps
or kneeling and raw,
        the entire, clenched town
tastes the floor.

Rain, Steam and Speed—
The Great Western Railway
after Turner

The weather's an eddying yellow, above and below. The windows the riders rely on—while hurtling miles, sequestered and dry—are wetter than sky.

Those passengers aspirate haze on the panes.

(Before planes, the only conception of fly
was through bird-watching, dreams, or a roof-flung goodbye.)

The damp unframed London's a wonder beyond. Behind: a storm.

Behind: the unwinding stories losses cause; the binding a promise obliges; the harms. Barbed wire on fences of farms.

The relentless memoirs the river writes of the dead.

(But forward. Ahead.
All metal; all move.)

Their imagined new lives are more real than the truth.

The straining train: all whistle, all wail. Beneath rails, a tiny canoe sways on swells, its rowers fogged down, unwell.

Farewell, oh horizonless evening.

(A crossing
is still a leaving.)

The Great Wave off Kanagawa
after Hokusai

The wave's gnarled fingers
reach, reach. The beach is nowhere.
We bow in the boats.

(*God of what floats, know us. God of water and wind, unbend the wave's rage.*)

The beach is nowhere.
We flee the bow, the boat
rows itself awry.

(*God of hands, brace our oar-grips. The grave's gnarled fingers wave, wave.*)

The silent snow falls.
The sky's white ghost rises, soars.
We grip our thin oars.

New York Movie
after Hopper

Is it depression or just senseless shoes that tempt the usher to rest against the wall, her eyes squeezed tight to mask the easy sprawl of limbs on the half-empty, cushioned seats?

She could be pensive; some young sorrow singing dirges in her head. Or simply stinging: maybe those black velvet straps slash burning rifts along her waning, pretty feet.

She leans. She lifts her fingers to her chin. She chose those groundless sandals to dispute the routine crudeness of her rough, blue uniform.

(But now her cheeks are crimson-stained and warm.)

She slumps beneath the quiet yellow light, while starlets laugh in perfect black and white.

The Persistence of Memory
after Dalí

>> Ripening is rotting.
Box and rock enact a basis.

> Clocks: negation, or its absence. Desert happening
unhappens.
All horizons: none the wiser.
>> Body: winding-
>>> clothed, all hiding.
Ants, so each an ampersand:
each & of things,
> each & again,
> the swarming always &
> until, then finally,
> an anyway,
> an ocean stilled;

>> an end.

Two Girls in Black
after Renoir

Overwhelming, the mourning this morning has brought.
The village alive with its grief for the lost.

The flocks of women don dark, grave frocks.
I sit for a moment, adrift in thought.

(But that somber silk funeral dress you just bought?
It looks grand, even though you're distraught.)

What horror, the cost of a life!
What strife, the finale awaits!

What terrible bedfellows
endings make for us all.

(But those tall, handsome suitors still call.
Foolish girl, to ignore what's here for what's gone.)

And autumn comes.
And the leaves will rot.

(But hope upon hope, he'll forget-you-not. Enough grief,
enough sullen and shudder and shut.

You're a vision in black,
you're a bud un-plucked.)

Yet the body is tucked in its bed.
(Yet the world's at the foot of your bed.)

And the corpse is still rouged and perfumed as a doll.
(But long summers transcend every autumn leaf's fall.)

As the widows wail funeral dirges....
(I'm in your head, whispering urges.)

I will silently, solemnly pray....
(But I'm here, and I won't go away.)

There's pain; there's dread.
(One day you'll wed....)

I'll grow frail and worn.
(You'll bask in bright sun.)

The hurt! *(The love.)* Distress! *(His kiss.)*
(What's the point if you only stop living?)

Blue Nude
after Picasso

Handless, and still your spited feet. All fetal, no reach. Beseech the inner elbow; the hell the whole world past the forearm offers. Remorseful. (*Oh, you are remorseful.*) Omissions by mouthfuls leading to caught. Clothes-less. Both men you love in another color. Both half-lovers. Both false places—(*one you are, one you want*)—half gone, half chalk. And not-so-faint black line of you keeps blue without from blue within. (*My sin, my monochrome.*) You feel alone, no eyes bloom in the shadows of your room but yours. You float, no floors, no doors in the office walls, hidden heavy hook of neck, crook of knee. (*Everyone hurts everyone but me.*) You most bereft of lucky girls. It's almost false: your everywhere arched cobalt over you—(*your inside, too*)—world washed, world glazed, and all around you dusk-hued cellophane of nameless aching.

Roman Notes
after Twombley

Wave at the words, are the words, words waving. Looped and looping, all writ wildly, strewn and misconstrued.	~~~~~~~~~~~~~~~ ~~~~~~~~~~~~~~~ ~~~~~~~~~~~~~~~ ~~~~~~~~~~~~~~~ ~~~~~~~~~~~~~~~	The shore responds. More than a problem: a scrawl. Illegible pleasure crocheted on dun-colored walls.
First, the swimming scribbled words make sense spinning through. Next, it's all just string across and scattered.	*(Beware: what's written does and does not matter.)* ~~~~~~~~~~~~~~~ ~~~~~~~~~~~~~~~	What's said, what crashes, whatever traverses. What waxes. What games. What falls in water, sometimes fails.
You can't read text if it's shattered.	~~~~~~~~~~~~~~~ ~~~~~~~~~~~~~~~ ~~~~~~~~~~~~~~~	There's a blackboard, first, then nails.

Ophelia
after Millais

A cloying offering: this summer's heat, the cheerful greenery deadheaded blooms leave, a leering gaze, a heart's alarming beat when greeted by her nearness. (*So, so soon, she'll come to fear this.*) All her woes are overthrown by dusk; its orange light, its perching on the cusp of something lovely. Breathing the musk and lily breeze eases her, belief seizing her: sweet air can only mean a sweeter meeting.

Until that evening. Slowly graying amber light. A lamp left lit for when he comes. But none of what he says is good. And none of the cautions she'd been warned of dulled his maddening, clanging anger. (*Nothing, none. He just gets himself gone.*) Deep into night, she laments what's lost. She runs to the river, she falls to the moss. The rough black tree's bark bears her up; she tentatively steps, collecting blossoms as she tiptoes, branch to branch, a nymph, a laugh that madly ricochets. Mourning what's alive and what decays. Beneath her, fallen flowers, bright and fragrant, rot in the water. They woo their fragile daughter down to the depths below. She gasps; she only grasps at rue. She does not rise. No rose, no jasmine coaxes her back home.

(*She dies alone.*)

Erased de Kooning
after Rauschenberg

(Remember me.
        Remember me.
The barely-snow. Our risk. White-breath.

                The lake looked like the sea.)

Acknowledgments & Notes

Special thanks to Susan McCabe, whose instruction on poem sequences was instrumental in shaping this collection. Also, of course, to my families: the Piazzas, Kranes and Jaroszewiczes.

"Café Terrace at Night" is for Elizabeth Cantwell and was first published in *Connotation Press: A Congeries*.

"School of Athens" is a cento; each line of the poem is a partial quote by one of the many artists and philosophers depicted in the Raphael painting.

"Rain, Steam & Speed: The Great Western Rail" is for Ryan Bender Murphy and was first published in *Forklift, Ohio*.

"New York Movie" is for Eric McHenry and was first published in a somewhat different form in *The Formalist*, and reprinted in *150 Contemporary Sonnets* (Evansville Press).

"Print Gallery" is for my husband Artur Jaroszewicz, the best person on earth.

"The Fight Between Carnival and Lent" was first published in *Prism Review*.

"The Great Wave off Kanagawa" is for Joshua Krane and Charles Ruggiero and was first published in *Mezzo Cammin*.

"Roman Notes" is for Joshua Rivkin and was first published in *Prism Review*.

"Blue Nude" is for Paula Mendoza-Hanna.

"Ophelia" was first published in *The Book of Scented Things: 100 Contemporary Poems About Perfume* (The Literary House Press).

Jessica Piazza is the author of two full-length poetry collections published by Red Hen Press: *Interrobang*—winner of the AROHO 2011 To the Lighthouse Poetry Prize and the 2013 Balcones Poetry Prize—and *Obliterations* (with Heather Aimee O'Neill, forthcoming). She holds a Ph.D. in English Literature and Creative Writing from the University of Southern California and is currently a contributing editor for *The Offending Adam* and a screener for the National Poetry Series. Her commitment to fostering writing communities wherever she lives led her to co-found *Bat City Review* in Austin, TX, Gold Line Press in Los Angeles, and Speakeasy Poetry Series in New York City. She teaches for the Writing Program at USC and the online MFA program at the University of Arkansas at Monticello.